Wolfgang Amadeus Mozart

Perspectives from His Correspondence

Studies in Austrian Literature, Culture and Thought

Translation Series

General Editors

Jorun B. Johns
Richard H. Lawson

Wolfgang Amadeus Mozart

January 27, 1756 – December 5, 1791

Perspectives from His Correspondence

by

Gloria Kaiser

English Translation by
Lowell A. Bangerter

Ariadne Press
Riverside, CA

Ariadne Press would like to express its appreciation to the Bundesministerium für Unterricht, Kunst und Kultur for assistance in publishing this book.

.KUNST

Library of Congress Cataloging-in-Publication Data

Mozart, Wolfgang Amadeus, 1756-1791.
  Wolfgang Amadeus Mozart : perspectives from his correspondence /
[selected] by Gloria Kaiser ; translated by Lowell A. Bangerter.
       p.   cm. -- (Studies in Austrian literature, culture, and thought.
Translation series)
  ISBN 978-1-57241-159-3
  1. Mozart, Wolfgang Amadeus, 1756-1791—Correspondence. 2.
Composers—Austria—Correspondence. I. Kaiser, Gloria, 1950- II.
Bangerter, Lowell A., 1941- III. Title.

ML410.M9A4 2007
780.92--dc22
[B]   2007014774

Cover Design
Art Director: George McGinnis
Illustration: Courtesy Österreichische Nationalbibliothek

Copyright 2007
by Ariadne Press
270 Goins Court
Riverside, CA 92507

All rights reserved.
No part of this publication may be reproduced or transmitted
in any form or by any means without formal permission.
Printed in the United States of America.
ISBN 978-1-57241-159-3

Contents

Foreword 3

The Letters 5

The Mozart Family 95

Chronology 99

Glossary 101

The antiquated language elements of the letters are virtually untranslatable. For that reason the letters were rendered from the "Mozart German" of the decades from 1760 to 1791 into contemporary German, and the translation into American English is based on that rendering. Obviously, care was taken to ensure that content, style, and vocabulary reproduce the atmosphere of the Mozart letters.

FOREWORD

"I cannot write poetically – I am not a poet. I cannot organize the expressions so that they yield shadows and light – I am not a painter. I cannot express my convictions and my thoughts through interpretation and through pantomime – I am not a dancer. But I can express my thoughts through sounds, for I am a musician." That was written by the twenty-one-year-old Wolfgang Amadeus Mozart to his father in November of 1777.

It seems to be a paradox to present Mozart as a writer, as a writer of letters, for the entire world knows this genius or believes that it knows this genius. After all, encyclopedias and lexica are filled with listings of his works and with interpretations and reviews. The musical vocabulary, the motifs and expressions have been scientifically decoded. In spite of that, the enigmatic element has remained and will remain, for the divine spark by which everyone is touched, which immerses itself in Mozart's music, does not yield itself to any scientific measurement – it exists, it is sensed, it is felt.

Who was the man who was borne through his life by that divine spark? A life that was strained and intensified, whether in pain or in happiness, to the utmost extreme; a life that conformed itself to no attempt to calendar it.

Childhood, youth, adulthood – how early Mozart was a finished human being in spirit and soul, finished and perfected for the path into that domain that lies beyond our measurability.

And that inner development of Mozart's personality is communicated to us through his letters, through correspondence.

The enumeration of dates and years is actually not important in that regard, for with Mozart almost everything happened too soon, too suddenly, before its time. The given dates are intended only to be guides and to call attention to the external European events into which the years of Mozart's life were embedded – for example, Marie Antoinette, while Mozart was in Paris with his mother, or the young Beethoven with Mozart in Vienna.

As is the case with every individual, in Mozart, too, lived many personae at the same time: the obedient son, the audacious cousin, the concerned brother, the loving husband. He was a friend to many people; he was above all an artist who fought for his freedom, who did not allow himself to be ordered around, even by an archbishop. Simultaneously he had to fight his way through mundane duties, was dependent upon commissions, suffered under intrigues, and was also a supplicant for money. All his life he was a traveler; Mozart was a cosmopolitan. Borders never meant anything to him; for him borders were only lines on the map.

During his life of not quite thirty-six years, heights and depths often did not follow one another but came at the same time; he was thrown simultaneously into the deepest despair and into the highest creative intoxication.

In his music he always sought and expressed simplicity and clarity; he avoided any romantic distortion – that was his claim to his reality.

The letters, the correspondence does not show us only historical facts, but opens for us door after door of the private chambers; and with that we learn the *truth of the heart* about the person, about the genius Wolfgang Amadeus Mozart.

Gloria Kaiser

To my relatives in Mannheim and Augsburg

I can finally report that on the 27th of January 1756, at around eight o'clock in the evening, my wife happily gave birth to a boy.

Today, the 28th of January 1756, we baptized him and gave him the names Johannes Chrysostomus Wolfgangus Theophilus. Using these baptismal names as a point of departure, his godfather Johann Theophilus Pergmayr recommended that we give our son the equivalent first names Wolfgang Amadeus for everyday usage.

Wolfgang Amadeus is healthy and strong, and taking the advice of the midwife we will nourish him with gruel and give him no mother's milk.

Everything else that this child brings us we will gratefully accept from the hand of God.

Your cousin, uncle, and brother,

Leopold Mozart
Court musician in Salzburg

From his father to his mother

Vienna, October 12, 1762

My dear Anna Maria!

Our four days in Schönbrunn are over and we are back in Vienna and are living in the inn *Zum falschen Kreuzer*. The innkeeper let us have a back room, because I wanted to spend only what was absolutely necessary for the three days' lodging. It is already quite cold in Vienna; for that reason the two children are sitting on straw mattresses and waiting, wrapped in blankets, until I return from seeing the publisher Artasani.
   The concert in Schönbrunn Castle was a beautiful success. Empress Maria Theresia was quite charmed by the children, and after the concert our Wolferl jumped up on the lap of the Empress and kissed her heartily. He also behaved like a gallant gentleman and courteously complimented little Marie Antoinette. He was really in love with the little princess who is the same age as he is. However, when he extended a marriage proposal to her, everybody laughed at him, even Nannerl. Our Wolferl was very disappointed about that and even depressed. 'Dear Tonerl,' he murmurs in his sleep. He will need a few more days to get over that disappointment.
   In general that is a characteristic of his nature that gives me cause for worry: when somebody approaches him affectionately, like the Empress or the little princess, when somebody directs a kind word to him or casually caresses him, then he would most like to give away his heart for such small bits of attention. And the disappointment that follows later almost throws him into a fever.

For that reason it is important that we use firmer discipline with him. He is now almost seven years old, and in accordance with the Jesuit education that I enjoyed, at the age of seven years he is considered to be an adult. It is sufficient if he kisses hands and offers compliments, but then he should go back to his sheets of music. Too much free time will be detrimental to his disposition.

Time is short and precious. Now they all want to see and hear the child prodigy, but who knows for how long?

Faithfully and lovingly yours,
Leopold

Postscript: With her eleven years Nannerl is already maternal enough to hug and warm her little brother. The children cannot do anything else, for the chamber has no windows and is dark. They sit and wait for me.

From his father to his mother

Brussels, May 31, 1763

My very dear Anna Maria!

Up until now I can report only hardships regarding this journey. First, the damage to the coach near Innsbruck. There the horses and coach got stuck in the mud because the roads were in terrible condition as a result of the melting snow. In any case the trip had to be interrupted for two days and two nights for coach repairs.

What was I supposed to do?! I had not planned anything for Innsbruck. Fortunately for us, the bishop's organist took pity on us, and during those two days I was able to explain the organ to Wolferl, and he was also able to play it. Thus the interruption of our trip was not a loss of time after all.

For the journey onward to Brussels I had to make a costly additional payment for our tickets. But for that Nannerl and Wolferl each had a separate seat and did not have to squeeze together on one seat. In Innsbruck I still thought that we would easily earn back those expenses.

But no! Now we have already been here for three weeks; I have walked my feet off, from the Bishop to the librarian, from the organist to the conductor. All for nothing. The Prince himself vowed that he wanted to listen to our children, but he did not name a specific day. Unfortunately, I have the worst impression of him. He does nothing but hunt, eat, and drink (one could certainly say: eat and drink to excess), and in the end it also turns out that he has no money.

The ladies here are very enthusiastic about our Wolferl. When we give a concert in a private house and he plays completely oblivious to the world, so totally entranced – you know that he plays divinely – then some of the noble ladies weep with emotion. And how often I have heard them say in recent days that his ability is incomprehensible.

That is right, but we must move on. For if neither money nor fame can be acquired here in Brussels, then onward to Paris.

Something else: The innkeeper served us a puree made of apples and grain for supper. Although it was sweetened with a large amount of honey, the acidic taste of the spoiled grain burned in our noses. The children ate it anyway. They were hungry. But the next day they had diarrhea and stomachaches. Everything is now alright again.

Of course I also thought of having a portrait painted. It went as always – Wolferl cannot hold still for a minute. The master became impatient, almost angry, and finally painted a portrait from memory. It is highly embellished and actually has little similarity to Wolfgang. But here I paid only half of what I would have had to shell out there at home in Salzburg.

Here is a hearty embrace from

Your husband,
Leopold

Postscript: It has been raining for a week and they are economizing in the use of wood everywhere, so that we can hardly dry our clothes.

To his mother

Paris, July 16, 1763

Dearest, best Mama!

The trip here was jolly, for it was warm in the coach and our coachman was a devil of a fellow who just raced along the roads with us.

I am writing to you personally, dear Mama, to show that I am thinking of you. Of course I will interrupt the letter several times, because I cannot write letters on paper as quickly as I can write musical notes.

Today I have a free afternoon, and I am sitting all alone in the chamber, which is equipped with elegant furniture. There is even a divan with silk bolsters. We are living at Monsieur Dubois's house. He is a violin maker and understands a lot about music, and above all he likes it when Nannerl and I play music. The man lives all alone. He is already quite far along in years, and he is gruff with his servants and probably all too strict. For that reason not even the water bearer remains in the house overnight. And then the taciturn man is alone with his violins.

Our dear Papa is on the go all day and always returns with good news. We give a concert almost every evening and our dear Papa organizes all of that!

Oh, our dear Papa really does come immediately after our dear God!

Now I must finally tell you that we were in Versailles! That is truly paradise – the flowers and the pergolas, fountains and pavilions, and the magnificent castle. Queen Maria Leszinski praised us very highly, and at the dinner that followed I was permitted to sit next to her and eat the soup and roasted chicken quite casually. There was also white cheese as well and dried, sweet grapes and crunchy bread that we dipped in honey.

Madame Pompadour was also present. She is very beautiful, blond, and tall. Nannerl and I were permitted to accompany her to her chambers. Full-length mirrors hang everywhere; the furnishings are gilded, and in every corner sit two or three servants who simply wait for a gesture from Madame, immediately jump up, and are at her service.

I do not think that the people who live in Versailles have much of an idea about life in Paris, for everything is quite different there. On the streets you see more beggars than anywhere else in the world. You cannot imagine at all, dear Mama, how poor the people of Paris are. We saw a man who was so weak that a stray pig gnawed at his hand; and the poor man could not defend himself, he was that weak. Everywhere there are enormous piles of garbage that are simply alive with rats. I shall not tell you about the smell at all, dear Mama. After a rain the streets are ankle deep in filth, so that those who must go on foot can only move along with the aid of wooden staffs or crutches, otherwise they would get stuck in the mire.

I cannot say whether or not the women of Paris are beautiful; even Nannerl could not tell you that, dear Mama. For most of the women have their faces painted so indecently that one can no longer recognize a face at all; and on their heads they have frameworks to which they fasten their wigs. Such is the fashion here.

But when the ladies and gentlemen appear as our audience, they show us great enthusiasm for our piano playing.

For that reason I like Paris very much, in spite of everything.

I kiss your hands a thousand times, dear Mama, and am

Your most obedient son
Wolferl.

From his father to his mother

Still in Paris, July 19, 1763

My beloved and faithful Wife!

A piece of good news! Listen to what Master Grimm, the secretary of the Prince of Orleans, writes in his magazine about our two children: "True wonders are rare enough. But a Salzburg music director just arrived here with two of the nicest children. The daughter, twelve years old, plays the piano brilliantly. Her brother, who will be eight years old next February, is such an unusual phenomenon that a person can

hardly believe what he sees with his own eyes and hears with his own ears. He immediately added the correct bass part to a minuet that I placed before him. And one evening he accompanied a female singer quite fantastically on the piano – the boy is a wonder!"
 Therefore, my dear, rest easy. We are doing well. We are very successful.

Your loving husband,
Leopold.

From his father to his mother

Lille, August 30, 1765

My dearly beloved Anna Maria!

 I can finally admit it to you. We have a few difficult days behind us. Nannerl was seriously ill; she had a fever and could hardly move any longer, so that I had to fear the very worst. For that reason I also summoned a priest and she received the last rites. Calm down while you read this. Everything turned out alright. Our Nannerl is already sitting diligently at practice at the piano again.
 Wolfgang became very upset about his sister's illness. You know, of course, that his frame of mind can easily become unbalanced. He cried and could hardly be consoled. But then he went into the next room and played the violin there; he simply improvised a few melodies, and from melody to melody Nannerl became calmer and healthier – at least it seemed that way.

In any case, in the next few days we will travel back to Paris, for no further orders for concerts can be expected from the Bishop here. Time is precious, and right now our children are still regarded as child prodigies; besides that they are used to working. They must never be permitted to become accustomed to leisure hours, for then my entire educational structure would collapse.

Continue to pray for us, that God's blessings may accompany us, and accept innumerable hearty embraces from

Your husband,
Leopold.

A postscript: Since we were always invited to dinner, there even remains a small profit from this stay. Nannerl is also so circumspect and usually asks at the dinner for two more pieces of bread to take along, and with that the children have their breakfast. Sometimes, however, the head waiters act like they do not understand and Nannerl gets nothing. Then we simply take apples, of which there are plenty here lying along the street. They are sweet and juicy; the apples are being harvested right now.

From his father to his mother

Vienna, October 18, 1766

My beloved Anna Maria!

What months of travel we have had to endure. At last we have arrived at our final stop – Vienna! Much has happened and changed as well; and I want to write to you about that, for Wolfgang, with his ten years, cannot yet grasp everything. He, too, will report to you, his view of the situation, of course.

Wolfgang no longer creates the stir anywhere, which we experienced four years ago. He has simply grown older. The people say: "Oh, it is the child prodigy again."

On some days Wolfgang is also rather sad about the fact that Nannerl stayed with you in Salzburg. But it is important that he learns to appear alone and to answer questions alone.

Good Master Grimm gave me a letter for the music publisher Artaria; perhaps a few of Wolfgang's sonatas will be published in his quarterly booklet. Grimm writes: "This boy is now ten years old. He has hardly grown at all, it is true, but he has made wonderful progress in music. He composes Italian arias and has such a profound knowledge of harmony and the most secret tricks of composing that it is unbelievable."

That all sounds very nice.

But we have rather difficult weeks and days behind us. Wolfgang was ill! He had a fever for a week and nobody could explain it. Neither tea nor vinegar compresses helped. And to my greatest alarm Baroness Waldstätten declared to me as well that smallpox is spreading in Vienna, but nobody speaks openly about it, in order not to drive the people into plague hysteria. On the seventh day of the fever Wolfgang suddenly could no longer see anything. I was in despair! But Heaven helped us!

Baron Waldstätten informed Franz Anton Mesmer, who is a theologian and physician, and he cured our Wolfgang with a magnet, hypnosis, and distilled water.

Wolfgang can now see again and is diligently at the piano as always.

How thankful I am to the Lord God.

The good Doctor Mesmer did not accept any honorarium at all, for he is a great music lover. He only wanted an "invitation for life" to all the concerts that Wolfgang will ever give in

Vienna. I was able to guarantee that to him, of course.

Now I no longer intend to hide from you what has changed for us in Vienna. After a concert the people want to have everything explained: why Wolfgang set the melody in this or that major key, or why he plays the cadences a sixteenth faster. As they walk away they often whisper: his father writes the compositions for him, and in reality he is not a child prodigy, but a poor, trained creature, and he has to earn a living for his parents.

It is actually music hell that we experience here. And they are so clever in devising intrigues. For example, they schedule a concert by Wolfgang at the very hour when the important members of the audience are invited to a ball at Prince Schwarzenberg's place – and then our Wolfgang plays for unoccupied seats.

All in all – the danger of smallpox and the disrespect here have strengthened my determination to depart immediately and return to Salzburg.

We must work out a new plan for Wolfgang and work in all seclusion in Salzburg for at least two or three years, and then continue with new travels.

By the way, in Amsterdam I bought him a frock coat made of dark red velour; it is too large for him. Rosl will have to alter it. And I also bought a wig, a used one. Wolfgang does not want to put it on because it makes his head itch; he claims that there are lice in it. Perhaps Rosl can begin weaving a wig out of flax in the meantime, for the people want to see Wolfgang as an adult, with a wig.

Hearty embraces from

Your faithfully loving husband,
Leopold

P.S.: Do not worry about the cold. The autumn is very mild in Vienna.

To his sister

Vienna, October 22, 1766

Dear Nannerl!

Do you immediately begin to cry when you see my handwriting? You should not do that; I have cried enough in recent weeks. I was ill and I missed you, I always miss you!

Now I intend to make you jealous, so I am going to tell you bluntly – all the ladies are enthusiastic about me. They say I am very attractive; above all, they are all infatuated with my hands. I receive all kinds of compliments about them.

Things are not going very smoothly with our budget, for our dear Papa and I cannot put together a ruffled shirt or polish our shoe buckles to the point that we can see our reflection in them. And the day before yesterday it would have been better if we had not eaten the bowls of large beans, because our bellies swelled up as a result, and then we performed a duet – you know what I mean. But Mama always says that it is better for the body to blow out the winds, than for them to build up in the head.

Tomorrow we are leaving, at last! And in a few days I will pinch you hard again if you do not make me a pan of egg dumplings.

With a thousand kisses and fillips on the nose,

Your loving brother,
Wolfgangerl

To his sister

Rome, June 15, 1770

Dear Nannerl!

You have no idea about St. Peter's Church. You get lost inside it; that is how big this cathedral is. And in this cathedral I stood across from the Holy Father, and he put the chain around my neck, and now I am a Knight of the Golden Spur!

During the meal that followed I sat between cardinals, and they encouraged me to improvise a few measures on the harmonium, as table music. That brought me much applause, especially from the ranks of the poor. For I must tell you, when Pope Clemens XIV invites people to dinner after a ceremony, then twelve families from the poor quarter of Rome are also invited. And these men and women sit with their children in long rows on a raised platform, so they actually look down on the Holy Father. I think that I should probably not be writing it like that now, but it was that way.

The meal itself was modest, to be sure, but every course was deliciously prepared – potatoes with butter, a soup with chicken, and white bread with honey for dessert. The foods were served on the most magnificent porcelain, and the water glistened in the crystal glasses. But the Holy Father himself ate from a wooden plate and drank from a stoneware mug; he did not even use eating utensils, but dipped his bread in the soup.

The day after tomorrow we will already be traveling on to Bologna.

With firm embraces,

Your brother,
Wolfgang

A postscript: It *is rather hot in Rome and our dear Papa and I are sweating terribly. I think that our clothing no longer smells good, or is it in the end we ourselves with the bad smell?*

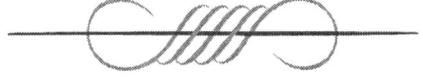

To his sister

Bologna, July 20, 1770

Dearest Sister Heart!

    You will not believe it, but here at the Leinlacher family's house everything is even finer than it is in the houses of the nobility. Everything is made of silver, even the chamber pots.
    Things are going very well for us here. Everyone has his own bed, completely equipped with feather pillows. And because our dear Papa feels so well in this environment, he said yesterday that he will look for a larger apartment for us in Salzburg. He says that it cannot go on this way, with us sleeping in disarray like the soldiers.
    From this decision of our dear Papa you can also read the fact that we raked in not only honor, but also beautiful, polished gilders.
    During the concert yesterday I caused a lady to moan! What do you say about your almost fifteen-year-old brother? Now I am beginning to seduce the ladies. When I have to lift my hand during a passage, in order to reach across the other hand, then that has an enormous effect. Yes, my hands are

simply beautiful. Just do not be envious, you dear Sister, you.
A thousand embraces from

Your brother,
Wolfgang

From his father to his mother

Bologna, July 31, 1770

My most dearly beloved wife Anna Maria!

Everything went well; the leather bag is full. I will be able to put away some gilders so that Wolfgang can now quietly compose again in Salzburg for one or two years.
In the meantime he has become an adult! Now he arranges his schedule himself, and when he is asked a question he speaks candidly – without coming to an agreement with me through glances. He has also brushed off his boy's voice. You will have to get used to the sonorous tone in which our son now speaks and sings.
Unfortunately, during the last few months he has still not grown. Let us hope that the good food at home will cause him to gain some height.
Be heartily embraced by

Your husband,
Leopold

To his sister

(Still) Bologna, August 5, 1770

My beloved Sister Heart!

    Now I must hurry with a few lines, for our dear Papa is already packing.
    For two days we have no longer been living with the noble Leinlacher family, but in a rather modest inn. The situation was this: the older daughter Rita fell passionately in love with my hands (or with me?) and continually wanted to sit at my side while I was composing, while I was playing the piano, even while eating. When her parents even endorsed that as well, our dear Papa decided that we would move.
    It was also better that way, because I felt so sorry for Rita, with her sad eyes, that I could not finish any work. During the last few days I have been able to catch up with everything – I am bringing four arias along, new Italian ones. You will be amazed. It is just too bad that at home in Salzburg they will again be sung by castrates because the archbishop does not tolerate women in the theater.
    You do not have to warn me about Thresel. Tell her that she is the best house maid and cook in the whole world. I dream of her cheese dumplings, and I am bringing along a basket full of stockings with holes in them, for dear Thresel is needed everywhere.
    With a thousand embraces from

Your brother,
Wolfgang

Postscript: Today I put on two pairs of stockings, one over the other, so that the holes are covered.

For our trip home we are taking the mail coach! That is cheaper, but the seats are without padding and when it rains the water streams through the slits in the canvas, do you remember? If I ever come into money, then I will only travel in the parlor coach anymore.

To his sister

Salzburg, May 15, 1772

My dear Sister, dear Nannerl!

There is so much to tell that I must finally write a long letter to you in Augsburg. For when you come back to Salzburg from your service in caring for our aunt, you will find many a change.

First the unimportant things: Yesterday there was a concert at Countess Lodron's place. The violin was played, or actually scratched at; it was horrible. For the Lodron woman had covered the piano with a rug for months, to protect it. And now, a few days before the concert it became apparent that this wonderful instrument is broken. For that reason, instead of piano tones there was scratching on the violin. In August, Countess Lodron wants to give a summer concert, and you, dear little Sister, are supposed to do the piano playing – if the instrument is repaired by then.

Now to the important things: The new Archbishop, Hieronymus Colloredo, has changed some things here. Our dear Papa is too modern for him, for example because of the Italian composition theory, about which Papa wrote a booklet. Besides, you know our dear Papa. He often wears his thorns directed outward. So in a conversation with the Archbishop, one word led to another, and Papa is no longer the conductor of the orchestra!

The Archbishop justified his decision with the argument that Papa travels around in the world with me too much and for that reason cannot properly fill the post of the Archbishop's orchestra conductor at all. Now money is very scarce here at home.

Our good Ignaz will remain with us, although Papa can no longer pay an errand boy. But Ignaz is of the opinion that better days will come again, and he will always get the water for us and take care of the stoves. Our worthy Thresel is staying in any case, although she burned the polenta while worrying about Papa's dismissal.

Now, of course, it would be important for me to obtain a fixed position; but there is nothing of the kind in sight. For that reason I am sometimes tormented by worries for hours, for how am I supposed to care for my parents if I have to tremble from one engagement to the next. So it is time for you to come home again soon, so that we can cheer each other up. I cannot compose when I am completely depressed by worries.

That is also why that affair with Roxane occurred. You know her, the daughter of Rosel, the laundress, the little girl with the blond pigtails. She is really nice and we really only embraced. But with her I could cry it all out without her asking in detail, why and how so.

Now you can imagine the story – her mother let out a scream, as if Roxane were now no longer a virgin. Everything got straightened out again, but those were rather nervous weeks and days.

Meanwhile I am again constantly at work, for while I am composing it is easiest for me to forget everything arduous around me.

My dear Sister Heart, come back to Salzburg soon. I pinch your behind and send firm hugs,

Your brother,
Wolfgangerl

To his sister

Salzburg, August 22, 1772

My dear Sister who is still in Augsburg!

You dear hussy, you! You probably do not want to leave your aunt at all anymore and come home! Now, however, you will be amazed: I am the Archbishop's concert master! With my sixteen years that is a good position!

Although we must tell the whole truth for what it is. The Archbishop appointed me to it in order to let our dear Papa feel his power even more – he dismisses the father; he enters a contract with the son. And he pays me an annual salary of 150 gilders, which is an insult, of course, because our dear Papa received ten times that much.

But I intend to swallow everything, for this is now the beginning of a fixed position. Papa already has travel plans for the coming year.

So come home soon, otherwise in the end I will already be gone when you come, and that would make me sorry, or don't you miss your brother at all?

Accept many thousands of embraces from

Your brother heart,
Wolferl

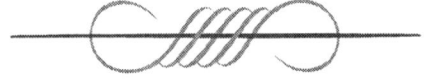

To his sister

Milan, April 14, 1773

Dearest Sister Heart!

It is enough to drive me to despair – once again things did not work out for a fixed position with the Grand Duke of Tuscany in Florence. Accordingly, we immediately traveled on to Milan and are lodging very comfortably with the Lauterbach family. However, it is very cold in the entire house, and they have too few bricks that we could use to warm our feet and put in our beds. My musical notation is often almost illegible because my fingers are so numb.

What you wrote about Schwarzbäcker's daughter Liesi, I foresaw exactly. Now she wants to enter a convent because of me! She is almost acting as if I, at the age of seventeen, had promised to marry her.

The dear Liesi has always wanted to enter a convent. Nothing happened between us. I gave her a dozen piano lessons, and because she really has no talent, and actually does not want to play at all, she quit – and if she says anything else, it is a lie and a deception.

We know, of course, the convents are overflowing with those daughters from noble houses who are too ugly or too stupid to be married off. And each of those prince's daughters brings a bundle of money with her into the convent. Thus it is naturally difficult for Schwarzbäcker's daughter to be accepted by the convent, unless she reconciles herself to scrubbing the floor for a decade – the pious life is expensive.

So, tell the good Liesi that she should stick to the truth, not continue to blame me, demand no money from our dear Mama, and wait like a good girl for her admission to the convent. Perhaps in the meantime a decent man will come and drive the longing for convent life out of her completely.

Dear little Sister, receive from me a thousand embraces, from now and into eternity, amen.

Your brother,
Wolfgang

Postscript: Since they are very seriously economizing on food in the home of the noble Lauterbach family, I have made friends with the kitchen maid (in all honor!), and yesterday she stuffed my waistcoat pocket full of freshly boiled potatoes. What a good soul! But Lord Lauterbach was amazed when smoke rose from my waistcoat pockets during the conversation with him. The potatoes were delicious.

To his father

Munich, May 16, 1774

Dearest Father!

Munich is a city in which I feel very comfortable. I am lodging with Count Seeau for a few weeks and am composing dance music and the music for his dinner parties for him; he always wants something jocular. With that I have earned myself three hundred gilders to date and have spent almost none of it because I am also invited to eat in the count's house.

Only I had to have two new frock coats and a pair of trousers made, but the house tailor used an old material belonging to the count for them, and although the velour has been turned, the pieces look quite decent.

I am having no luck with the church authorities here either. Half a dozen times I tried to see the Bishop of Chiemsee, and when I finally stood in front of him, he said to me, "Ah, Mozart, the first thing for you to do is become famous, then we will see. You must understand that here in Munich people do not want to deal with beginners. So travel and become famous!"

What should I have answered to that? I am eighteen years old and neither famous nor a beginner.

Now you can imagine how happy I am about the commissions of Count Seeau.

With a thousand hand kisses I am

Your obedient son,
Wolfgang Amadé

To him from his father

Salzburg, August 28, 1774

My dear Son!

During recent weeks I have spent many sleepless nights worrying about your future.

Now read and listen:

As a result of the bishop's words, your vanity has been

hurt, to be sure, but you do not recognize that he sees your situation correctly. Become famous! Not until you have a famous name will you attain fixed employment, and that is what you need for your future.

But what do you do?! You make yourself small, sell yourself for a pittance to a Count Seeau, and are happy with praise and beautiful words, for which neither an innkeeper nor a coachman will give you anything.

I had to raise seven hundred gilders to pay for your travel expenses, and you are writing dance music! Soon you will be faced with nothing! And think about the fact that where there is no money there are also no friends.

I had to give vent to my feelings at last and remind you that you do not live alone in this world. Your sister is supposed to establish a household – from what? She is 23 years old and does not want to enter a convent.

So request more money, and depart from Munich if nothing more can be obtained.

I embrace you warmly.

Your worried father

To his sister

Munich, December 30, 1775
(It is bitterly cold; the frostwork on the window flourishes centimeters thick)

My dear Nannerl!

I shall be happy and relieved when the church bells ring in

the New Year. This was a zero year, this year of 1775!

First I wait for five months for a fixed position with the Archbishop and I achieve nothing; then in addition to that he has the theater closed.

Believe me, Nannerl, since I have been back in Munich things have gone better for me, because I do not constantly see and sense the harsh steps and looks of our father.

What am I supposed to do? I worked enough. On Christmas Eve I counted up the works I wrote this year; there are more than a hundred of them – serenades, violin concertos, piano concertos, and of course the etudes for my female students.

But now I want to stop my complaining and come to something amusing. Tell Miss Mitzerl that she should not doubt my love. I always have her sweet face before my eyes. And to the chubby-faced Helene you had best say – the same thing. After all, the two girls do not know each other. There are also very pretty girls here in Munich, and I have several of them as students. One of them is Gisela; she has eyes like a bouquet of violets and she is very shy; she begins to stutter when she is supposed to talk with me. The name of another one is Ida; she is saucier. She sometimes places her hand wrong to catch hold of my hand.

Oh, Nannerl, everything takes place in all innocence. I tell you about my everyday life, which consists of giving lessons and composing and playing music. And I beg of you – not a word about my students to our father. I already know, at the age of almost nineteen I should behave more seriously.

Receive from me a thousand wishes for a good, much better year of 1776 and be firmly embraced by

Your brother,
Wolfgang

To the Archbishop of Salzburg

Salzburg, June 15, 1777

To His very noble Grace, Archbishop Hieronymus Colloredo!

Most humbly I permit myself in all brevity and without long circumlocutions, frankly and freely, to inform the Lord Archbishop of the following:

Very noble Archbishop, some months ago you denied my father's request for leave and had me notified that the son, in other words I, should travel alone, because I am only one fourth in your service.

I want to do that, more precisely as a completely free artist, as a man who is free of *all* responsibilities.

You already told me once that I should seek my fortune somewhere else, if I did not like it in Salzburg. Fine, I shall do that now, and I shall go to Paris for several months and afterward I shall travel to somewhere else.

I will not enter your service so readily again. My dear mother will accompany me to Paris, so you will not need to tremble about the salvation of my soul.

It does say in the gospel that the children, the more talents they have received from God, have to care for the wellbeing and the future of their parents, and naturally for their own livelihood. I shall abide by all of that, as an obedient and loving son, but also with all of my love for my work.

I send you my regards.

Your former conductor,
Wolfgang Amadeus Mozart

To his sister

Salzburg, June 20, 1777

Placed on the pillow of my dear sister Nannerl!

    How else am I supposed to speak with you when the walls have ears in our home? Do not weep too much about my travel plans. You must realize and understand that I had to free myself from the Archbishop. I will not let myself be treated like a snot-nosed boy. He gave me only a part of a fixed position and a gratuity as a salary – no!
    And please, comfort our father. Perhaps he believes that he has now lost his influence over his obedient son. It is not that. But I had to determine my own course at last.
    I also ask you to starch my frilled shirts with a lot of rice starch, for en route it is difficult to find a good laundress.
    With a thousand brotherly kisses,

Your brother,
Wolferl

From his father

Salzburg, September 25, 1777

My dear Son!
    Two days ago you left with your dear Mama, and worry and grief at parting put me in bed for a day. Everyone here in

the house suffers in his own way from your absence. Nannerl vomited for an entire day; Thresel bakes doughnuts and in doing so uses too many eggs and too much flour, but you know that against a black mood (that is what she calls her sadness) she knows no other prescription but cooking and baking. And our good Ignaz sits before the front door and blows soap bubbles into the air; when he is especially successful with one, he jumps up and shouts: "Fly after them!"

It is very foggy in Salzburg and too cold for the season. I have already wrapped my fur around my shoulders; otherwise I could not write because of the cold. In the evening I will play a game of chess with Nannerl, and tomorrow I will give lessons to Countess Henriette Arco.

I shall not give you any advice in this letter. You are an adult and I trust in the blessings of God. Be heartily embraced by

Your father.

Postscript: I am enclosing with the letter the music paper that just arrived. They have never before sent us such fine and smooth paper. Pay attention to your health and do not sniff too much tobacco.

To his father

Munich, October 9, 1777

Mon très cher Père! [My very dear Father!]

We could hardly wait to arrive in Munich, for the journey was terrible. Those carriages ram the soul out of a person! The seats are as hard as stone. I did not think that I would get my rear end here whole; it is fiery red, although I held my hands between my behind and the seat for hours.

We are lodged well, to be sure, but in spite of our thriftiness we use a lot of money. For every jug of water that he brings for the wash basin, the house boy holds his hand out. And the maid would like a whole gilder for every piece of wood! They all believe that I am a wealthy man because the messenger from the Bishop brought a letter for me to the house. In it, however, there was only one of his delays.

But do not worry, dear Father, I shall not let myself become discouraged. And today I shall yet buy a basketful of wooden shavings from a carpenter. We must have it warm, for my dear mother cannot wait for me in the cold room, and I cannot work in the cold.

There is nothing more to report. Do not worry.

With a thousand hand kisses I am

Your obedient son,
Wolfgang.

To his cousin Maria Anna Thekla Mozart

Munich, October 10, 1777

Very dearest Cousin!

It was a stroke of luck that after so many years we saw each other again. Already as children we were a merry team. But now you are a respectable young lady and I almost do not know how I should address you.

I actually want to write something clever, but nothing clever occurs to me. Only one thing is certain, I shall never write you a serious letter. I want to be really childish with you again.

Do not forget to remind the dean to send me the sheets of music. In the near future I shall write you a letter in French, and you can have it translated into German. Have you finally started to learn French?

You asked me the most diverse things. Now, I want to tell you a secret: with Lieserl, Elisabeth, I began to sin – unfortunately it is already over. But I admit that sin and I admit further, that I enjoyed it, and that I hope to improve myself in my sinful life, which I have just begun. That is the entire solemn truth, and I live in the firm confidence that I am not a bad person because of it.

You see, now I have confessed to you.

I kiss your cheeks and your hands a thousand times.

Your cousin,
Wolfgang Amadé

To his cousin Maria Anna Thekla Mozart

Mannheim, November 15, 1777

Ma très chère Cousine! [My very dear Cousin!]

You answered my last letter so beautifully that I do not know where I should get the words to express my thanks to you for it. You want to know how I like Mannheim? As well as one can like a place without his little cousin.

Pardon my poor handwriting; the quill is already old and quite worn-out. That is the difference – I have been sh... from the same hole now for almost 21 years and it has not torn yet.

Oh, what a blessing it is, that I can be so truly dumb and childish with a person in all confidence. You already understand everything in the right, good-natured sense.

Now I have to stop because I am not dressed yet, and we are going to eat right away, so that afterward we can sh... again – that is simply how it goes. Do you still love me? I assure you once again that I am

Your most obedient servant and sincere cousin,
Wolfgang Amadi

A postscript: Do not be shocked about my coarse expressions. For you know that I only speak that intimately with you – with everyone else I speak very seriously and like an adult.

To his sister

Mannheim, February 2, 1778

Dear Sister Heart!

A few days ago I gave a concert at the home of Princess Charlotte von Oranien. She is a lover of arias, so I wrote two of them for her. In her orchestra she also has a very young singer with a heavenly voice – Aloisia, Luise is her name. She is only sixteen years old, but with her voice, with her gracefulness, she could be a prima donna at any theater. In any case, for that reason my stay here in Mannheim becomes more pleasant for me every day.

Munich was the way it always is, from the Bishop nothing but promises; to him I am still a long way from being famous enough for a position under contract. And the Elector of Mannheim also offers only hopes, but nothing else.

In Augsburg I teased my dear cousin Anna Maria Thekla. We are now in lively, childish correspondence. Our good little cousin has become plump; that suits her well. While dancing she is soft to hold – do not be shocked, we only danced two minuets anyway. She sends you greetings and kisses. Out of pure respect for your beautiful piano playing she does not have the courage to write you a letter.

But now to the main thing that I want to discuss with you – Aloisia Weber. She lives very modestly with her parents and her three sisters in the customhouse. Her father is a thoroughly honest man who earns only a little money as a music copyist and assistant municipal secretary. Of her mother they say that she is very ambitious and therefore sometimes somewhat caustic. I cannot confirm that, for she is friendly to me; she even repairs my frock coats.

But those are all trivialities.

When Aloisia, Luise and I make music together, we feel only unity. I wrote an aria for Aloisia, and when she sings that aria, she almost makes the notes glitter with her voice – do you understand? It sounds then as if we had tormented ourselves for days with practice and study, while everything flows very easily, from my hands, and from Luise's throat – and I feel like I am in heaven.

My very dearest Sister, now you can imagine that I would most prefer not to travel on from Mannheim at all. I hope that our dear Mama has not yet sent an announcement of my intentions in that regard to Salzburg. Perhaps you can help

clarify some things to our father, the old man.
    With a thousand embraces from
Your brother,
Amadeus.

Postscript: The snow that has been falling for days has made all the roads impassable; not even the horse-drawn sleds get any further, so I tromp along on foot. You can imagine what this cold February consumes with respect to the cost of wood.
Second postscript: There is even a coffeehouse here; the smells and the smoke there are so oriental that you think you are in Turkey.

To his cousin Maria Anna Thekla Mozart

Mannheim, February 10, 1778

My dearest little Cousin!

    Now it is time that I let my childlike soul express itself freely for a few lines and talk with my dear little cousin. You will perhaps believe that I have died. But how could I write so beautifully if I were dead? I have had so much to do that although I did have time to think about my little cousin, I did not have time to write, so I did not do it.
    About the sonata, Miss Freysinger will still have to be patient for a little while. Yes, if it were a sonata for you, for my dear little cousin, it would have been finished a long time ago. But really! Besides, if it would at least earn me a bag of coins, that, too, would be something different. In the end Miss Freysinger will want to barter, and I do not permit bartering,

because I am not a woman.

So sleep well and stretch you're a... out toward the moon. My regards to your lord producer (father) and your lady producer (mother), namely to the man who made the effort to create you and the woman who let it be done to her. Farewell, dearest Cousin, and remain bound to me in friendship.

I remain eternally

Your sincere friend,
Wolfgang Amadé.

From his father

Salzburg, February 20, 1778

My dear Son!

I almost have difficulty in conveying my thoughts to you in an orderly manner, because worry about your future has brought my mind into such great turmoil. To be sure, your mother wrote me that everything is taking the best course with you – she wanted to reassure me.

However, from Augsburg, from your uncle, my brother, quite different reports reached me.

So, in sequence:

The whole world knows that you have a good heart, and through working exclusively with music you live somewhat apart from the real world. With pretty words and kindnesses one can easily turn you in any direction, and then you are used by some people for their own fame and purposes. You do not seem to notice that at all!

But you owe your parents help and devotion in every form. For that reason your journey has to have only *one* meaning, *one* goal, to obtain a permanent position at last, or to travel to another city where you can expect a higher salary. With your earnings you have to support your parents and also your sister.

Do you want to remain a little musical artist whom the world forgets? Do you want to become a music copyist who trembles waiting for commissions? Do you want to remain an unknown man who lives in poverty with a wife and a room full of children on a few sacks of straw? I did not take such pains with you for that, and I did not put all our money into your travels and your robes for that. You should become a famous concert master and composer, one whom people read about in books. And you have to live exclusively toward that goal.

And what do I hear?! Everywhere, in Munich, in Augsburg, you have your little "scenes," your love affairs. Fine, that is natural at your age of twenty-two. But now this girl! She is a girl of sixteen! You write arias for her, have her mother mend your clothes – this Aloisia Weber has driven you out of your mind!

No!

Away with you to Paris!

I have written a separate letter to your dear mother. She will read to you all of the instructions for the journey to Paris. For although the news of your lifestyle put me in bed, I anticipated everything and have also already written to Master Grimm in Paris, so that the doors leading to the important people will be open for you.

Make money and fame for yourself in Paris. Forget that little singer – that will pass.

And think of your father, who, at the age of 59, can no longer endure many reports of that kind about your naïve good nature.

With firm confidence in your obedience, I embrace you.

Your father

His mother to his father

Paris, March 23, 1778

My most dearly beloved Husband, dear Leopold!

It is snowing and the room is cold and as dark as a dungeon. I can hardly read the words that I am writing. And I am writing because I am already afraid that I will forget how to talk. That is how alone I am all day.

Our Wolfgang truly has no luck here. He is out of the house all day because one cannot set up a piano in this hole of a room. Everything is too confined. He is permitted to play and compose at Master Grimm's place. And every day he presents himself to the most diverse nobility, and then in the evening he comes home hungry and without any commissions. The people of Paris are interested only in extravaganzas; and years ago Wolfgang was still an extravaganza, as a child prodigy!

Yesterday he went to the Countess Chabot's home. He waited for hours in an ice-cold room; then he played on a miserable pianoforte with fingers that were stiff from the cold – and the ladies and gentlemen did not listen to him at all, but played cards while he was performing.

He did not even receive dinner as a reward. They applauded, thanked him, and the countess gave him a letter of recommendation for Count Sickingen.

He will have to give even more lessons so that we can buy our daily potatoes, and I will try to knit; then the dark hours of the day will pass more quickly.

I want to mention one other thing. After the farewell from Aloisia Weber, Wolfgang was ill for several days; he had a fever. Now he no longer talks about her; that is over – hopefully.

With a thousand embraces,

The woman who is married to you,
Anna Maria

To his father

Paris, April 17, 1778

Dearest Father!

Now I am here after all, and specifically in fulfillment of my obedience to you, and unfortunately I am unable to find good fortune. Paris has changed. One cannot earn money here in an honest way. I do not want to write to you at all how often I have already played for armchairs and walls, and afterward I had to argue about a few coins.

My symphony, which I composed during my very first days here, was performed so horribly that I did not recognize it again at all. The notes were played and scratched so sloppily that I left in the middle of the concert. Supposedly there was a lot of applause; should I believe it? I have not received any other commission.

Meanwhile, the good Master Melchior Grimm no longer belongs to the modern group. That means that those people whom Master Grimm recommends to me have small salons and never a large audience. Here they talk about Christoph Willibald Gluck and Niccolo Piccinni! Parties have formed in that regard. The man who goes to a Gluck concert is never seen at a Piccinni concert.

And I am left with the compliments, but nothing else. Whether a count, a prince, or a baron, they make an appointment with me for a certain day, then I play, and they promise – and that is that. A person who does not live here cannot imagine at all the dissipated life that is lived here.

The stink in the streets is bestial. In the coaches they have closed the lace curtains so that they do not see the filth, and if a person has to walk on the street, he holds a perfume bottle in front of his nose.

In spite of all that, I intend to endure it for a while longer; things really must turn in my favor.

I kiss your hands a thousand times and am

Your obedient son,
Wolfgang Amadeus

To Miss Aloisia Weber

Paris, April 17, 1778

My *carissima amica* [dear friend], dearest Miss Aloisia!

For today I have fulfilled my duty as a son and have written my father a report. But I shall not let go of this packet of mail without writing a few lines to you: I think of you constantly, dearest Luise.

I actually do not have any more than that to say, for the idea of constantly thinking contains everything, of course; you will understand that correctly, and just as soon as I have accomplished anything at all here, perhaps a commission for an opera or a major symphony, then I shall stick myself to the chair, work day and night, and in a jiffy I shall be with you again in Mannheim.

So do not forget that I am always thinking about you, dearest Luise. Looking forward to our reunion is my entire and my only consolation in these dull and dismal days and weeks.

I bow full of compliments and am in all honesty

Yours,
Wolfgang Amadeus

To him from his father

Salzburg, May 20, 1778

My dear Son!

Hopefully you have freed your mind of the matter of Aloisia Weber. You are so susceptible to flattery and for that reason you do not grasp the fact that this person wanted to make her fortune through you. She would only have used you to become a famous singer through the singing of your arias. And add to that her family, those Webers, three daughters are still waiting to be supported.

Work, do not miss any opportunity to play for the right and important people.

May God's blessings be upon you! And accept hearty embraces from

Your father

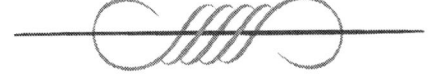

To his sister

Paris, June 4, 1778

Dear Sister, very dear Nannerl!

You will already know from talking to our father, as a result of our correspondence, that nothing is going as he imagined here in Paris. It is also impossible to communicate to him the details of the adversities, for when you sit at home in orderly circumstances you cannot imagine some things at all.

Yesterday, for example, I played in Count Rodunay's salon; even Madame Marie Jeanne Dubarry was present, and she is still very powerful in society as the former mistress of the Emperor. I reaped moderate applause, even compliments, and they gave me steamed plums and anise bread to eat – they paid me nothing at all! And I, stupid ox that I am, went to the extra trouble of composing a rondo and gave that sheet of music to Madame Dubarry, instead of wax flowers. She raved about my mystical hands, as if that did anything for me.

The deficit of that evening, however, was not complete until I was at the house gate, for then the coachman wanted double the fare because of the thunder storm. I almost got into a fight with him. I lay awake last night – it cannot go on this way. I do not see open doors for me anywhere.

It is also the fact that since dear Marie Antoinette has been queen, they no longer like the Austrians here; they are skeptical about all German speakers in general. For here it is the way it is everywhere. When the people have to live in misery they need a guilty party. It is easier to blame a single individual than a class, like the noble class here, for example. The dear Marie Antoinette lives in Versailles and actually has no idea how badly things are going for the people. You probably still have the most beautiful memories of Versailles, everything of gold, crystal, and mirrors, and Marie Antoinette spends her life there. Every noble family wants to act like the royal family, so they overtrump each other with the most expensive robes and pieces of jewelry. For that reason even the nobles must economize more and more to support their lifestyle, and they economize in the concerts and the composition commissions. Now the latest thing is that the spectators – and all of them are nobles as well – pay a leather bag full of coins for a seat on the stand at Versailles. For anyone who has not sat on the stand in Versailles at least once a year and watched the king and queen at their midday meal is a nobody in Paris society. Those are the customs here.

By the way, Nannerl, there is also gossip about something discrete. Just imagine poor Marie Antoinette. She has been married for eight years, but in the actual sense of the word she has been so for only a year. Do you understand? Her husband, King Louis XVI, had a problem in that respect. They are whispering that our Empress, Maria Theresia, in despair about the posterity that did not appear, even sent her son Josef to Versailles a year ago to speak serious words to King Louis XVI, that is to say, the husband.

In that regard I naturally cannot stifle the observation – if the dear little blonde Antoinette had accepted my marriage proposal back then in Schönbrunn, she would not have had this problem.

My beloved Sister Heart, now I have told you extensively how things are going here in Paris.

I will also say quite candidly, and that, of course, only to you, dear Sister, that after the paternal reprimand that I had to endure because of my beloved Aloisia, I shall, to be sure, maintain the ritual of the obedient son, but internally I have laid out a different path for myself. It has simply been ordained by Heaven that I desire an understanding father and have an entirely different father.

Take good care of our father and do not tell him a word of my thoughts. I would be very happy to receive a few lines from you, or have you already forgotten me, you hussy.

Receive my heartiest embraces,

Your brother,
Wolfgang

To his father

Paris, July 3, 1778

Mon très cher Père! [My very dear Father!]

How am I supposed to find the words? My mother passed peacefully away in God at about ten o'clock this evening. God gave her to us; He could also take her from us.

How will you, my dear Father, and how will my sister live with this news?

During the last three days my mother was delirious with fever and gradually lost her awareness. I held her hand and spoke to her, but she did not hear me. She lay there that way until she died.

I prayed almost unceasingly during the past few days, and when she got worse and worse I asked the Lord God for two things: for a good hour of death for my mother, and for courage and strength for myself. The kind Lord God heard my prayer and gave me those two blessings.

As I watched her pass away like that, I felt a powerful desire to be able to go with her, and thus I also came to understand that she has only gone on ahead of me and us. That gave my soul much comfort. My mother's time had run out, the Almighty wanted her. In such circumstances, no matter what all the doctors may say, nothing else could have been done. The Almighty made his decision and we have to submit to it.

Your obedient son,
Wolfgang Amadeus Mozart

From his father

Salzburg, October 2, 1778

My dear Son, dear Wolfgang!

The pain caused by the fact that your mother, the wife that I loved more than anything, no longer lives, will never diminish. I shall learn to live with it. At the same time I am grateful to God that I was permitted to experience the happiness of finding the person who was intended for me. We waited for each other for almost seven years until we were finally able to obtain the blessing for ourselves in the year 1747. When I think about how casually, even disparagingly the word *love* is used for every little scene and advance. Love — we, your mother and I, were borne up by that all-inclusive divine grace for almost thirty-one years.

And completely in accordance with the wishes of your dear mother, we will continue to make an effort to obtain a position for you. I wrote to Master Grimm. He will advance you the money for your departure. Wolfgang, come home to Salzburg; I can possibly negotiate a position for you as court organist. Here in Salzburg you will have your order. You will be amazed at how conscientiously Nannerl governs the household. Everything is clean as a whistle. She has even taught Ignaz how to churn butter.

Perhaps you can also make a stop in Munich. The little singer, that Aloisia Weber, is now singing at the court theater in Munich. Count Spaur, the director of the court theater, wrote me that. But I think that will no longer interest you.

Travel soon. We are looking forward to you.

Your father

To his father

Strassburg, November 3, 1778

Dearest Father!

I departed from Paris as quickly as I could, naturally without leaving any debts behind. In order to save money I bought a cheap ticket on a large coach – that was thoughtless of me. For that spacious vehicle took ten days for the stretch from Paris to here, and some of the other passengers in it spat and farted. It was terrible.

Tomorrow I will immediately travel on to Munich. From there I will send you word again.

We want to look forward; my dear mother would also have wanted it that way.

I kiss your hands a thousand times.

Your obedient son,
Wolfgang

Johann Becke to Mozart's father Leopold Mozart

Munich, November 25, 1778

Dear Conductor Leopold Mozart!

You will wonder about the return address – may I introduce myself: Johann Becke, flutist in the court orchestra of the Munich Theater and a brotherly friend of your son Wolfgang.

He does not know that I am writing to you, but I see it as my friendly duty to inform you.

As he announced to you, Wolfgang arrived here in Munich on the 10th of November.

May I take the liberty of telling you that it was easy to discern what bait you used to lure your son away from Paris – Aloisia Weber. When Wolfgang read in your letter that Aloisia was singing in Munich, no coach could be fast enough for him, in order for him to see his beloved Aloisia again at last.

Unfortunately, Mademoiselle Aloisia has completely changed in her attitude toward your son. She spoke indifferently and condescendingly to him and called him a little, unemployed music conductor who could never help further her career!

I cannot repeat at all, what injuries and wounds that mademoiselle gave to my best friend Wolfgang – she trampled around on his heart. And that is why I am writing to you. For after his last conversation with Aloisia, Wolfgang was so heart-stricken that he fled to my house and lay in bed for four days with a fever.

Wolfgang loved Aloisia, and I think that when it is a matter of the divine message of love, we human beings should not interfere.

Please pardon my open words, dear Conductor Leopold Mozart. But your son has a good heart and he was severely disappointed and injured. I beg of you, take that into account when you make new plans for him. Then he himself would never have the courage to be disobedient to you, even in only the smallest thing.

I bow to you full of respect,

Johann Becke, a friend of your son Wolfgang

To his father

Munich, December 31, 1778

Dearest Father!

    With today's date this horrible year comes to an end. You probably know, in the next few weeks Aloisia Weber will marry the famous actor Joseph Lange and go to Vienna with him, and there, through the protection of Mr. Lange, become a famous person in a short time. Fate wanted it that way.

    Too bad, thus everything remains uncertain for me. How beautiful it would be if I had the certainty of also being loved by the one and only person that I love.

    What is left to me is my work, and slowly I am getting back into my daily rhythm. My mood is dark, to be sure, but I will keep all of my pains to myself. That is why I am writing you this letter, because I do not want to talk about it in Salzburg.

    With a thousand hand kisses,

Your obedient son,
Wolfgang

To his friend Johann Becke

Salzburg, March 5, 1779

My dear, best friend Johann!

At last I find the words to thank you. How you looked after me during my days of fever in Munich. Only now, after so many weeks and months, am I able to think about the incidents and conversations with Aloisia without becoming unable to work for half a day because of mourning and agony of soul.

What a vulgar character that woman is. In February of 1778, at my departure for Paris, she cried and swore to be true to me – what a laugh! A few months later she criticized the scars on my face; she did not like the buttons on my musician's waistcoat because they were not gold, and then I was also too short for her! If she was looking for a tall man, she should never have gone walking with me. By the way, that Mr. Lange is also at most five centimeters taller than I am. And she also knew from the beginning that I am not a famous man. It was all lies and deception; she kept me waiting and lured a few arias out of me. She sang those beautifully and now she has a career.

Oh, the girl that does not want me can kiss my a... – I often sing that to myself.

Now added to the blows to my heart is also the humiliation at the fact that my father anticipated all of that – I cannot say anything at all to that.

I do not have to explain these feelings to you, of course. You feel the way I do in everything, and for that I embrace you very heartily.

Remain my friend.
I am bound to you in eternal friendship,

Yours,
Wolfgang

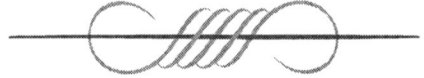

To his sister

Vienna, February 6, 1781

Ma très chère soeur! [My very dear Sister!]

    From our dear father's last letter I learned that you are ill, and that causes grief and worry for me. Now I want to write to you in all honesty: The best cure for your perpetual indisposition would be a man. And because I am convinced that a husband will have such a great impact on your health, I wish with all my heart that you will soon be able to marry.
    Just what is the situation with that Franz Yppold? He would really have to find a position for himself here in Vienna. And you could give piano lessons and would earn yourself the necessary money that way. And we could also bring our father to Vienna and all three of us could live happily. So, do not be bashful, but do talk to Yppold. As a member of the Royal War Council he is accustomed to direct talk.
    I send you a thousand kisses and am

Your dear brother,
Wolferl

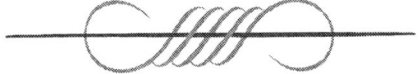

To his cousin Maria Anna Thekla Mozart

Vienna, March 4, 1781

Ma très chère Cousine! [My very dear Cousin!]

    At last I can write you a juicy letter again.
    Tomorrow I am leaving for Munich. Dearest Cousin, do not be a little bunny, but come to Munich, too. Then I shall take you around everywhere. At the theater you will receive a major role to play. Obviously I will compliment you, kiss your hands, and shoot with both barrels.
    So, my angel, my heart, I await you with anguish. I do not want to report anything about myself. During recent months there have been too many annoyances with my honorable patrons. I would be happy about a letter from you, or is a letter to me not worth the postage? Now farewell, dearest Cousin. I remain eternally

Your sincere cousin and friend,
Wolfgang Amadé Mozart

To his father

Vienna, May 1, 1781

Dearest Father!

 My friend Schidenhofer really could have told me that he intends to marry. I wish him happiness with all my heart. Although, that is once again a marriage for money and I do not want to marry that way. I want to make my wife happy and not attain my happiness through my wife. For that reason I also want to enjoy my freedom until I can support a wife and children. It is already clear to me that for Schidenhofer it was necessary to take a wealthy wife; that is how it is with the nobility. Those nobles never marry out of gusto and love, but only for self-interest and all kinds of secondary purposes. It would be something if those individuals, who have everything anyway, could also even choose a wife that they loved! That is the privilege of us poor people. We have nothing to lose, no reputation, and we have all our wealth in our heads. So nobody can take our wealth from us, and we can take the wife who suits us!
 I shall write a separate letter of congratulations to Schidenhofer. Unto you, dearest Father, I remain

Your obedient son,
Wolfgang Amadeus

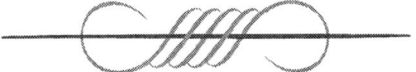

To his father

Vienna, May 10, 1781

Dearest Father!

I spent the entire night thinking, in order to put the events of recent days in order, and now I want to communicate them to you. For that reason, please prepare yourself for a lengthy letter. Some events cannot be described in a couple of lines.

Father, you know that I only came back to Salzburg more than a year ago to please you. For the proud noblesse of the Archbishop has been unbearable for me for a long time, and if I had had my way, I would have wiped my behind with the Archbishop's last decree – pardon me. He threw a beggar's pay at me, and I swallowed that. In addition, I swallowed the fact that the Salzburgers, including the Archbishop, make it clear to me again and again – just why did Mozart return from Paris? Anybody who does not like it in Salzburg can stay away. The trip to Vienna came very opportunely, of course. I wanted to make important contacts in the Hofburg Palace and become personally acquainted with the new Emperor, Josef II.

The political reason for this visit, of course, does me no credit – the Archbishop of Salzburg is making a polite visit to the new Emperor in Vienna and for that purpose is taking his musicians along. We have to obey the Archbishop like lackeys, and that is exactly how we have been treated in recent weeks.

When they served dinner at noon, I sat with the cooks at the side table along with the valet and the water bearer. The Archbishop dined, laughed, and discussed things with the diplomats and secretaries, and I, a few arm lengths distant from him, sat there as silent as a carp, for not a single person talked to me. And of course they also economized with the food for the musicians. If, for example, there was rabbit in cream sauce for the Archbishop, I had the rabbit's head served to me in a thin soup. And just where is a person supposed to begin gnawing on a rabbit's head? For the evening meal we received three ducats. That does not go a long way; it is at most enough for a bowl of gruel and a piece of bread.

So on the second day I was already beginning to work toward my independence. An offer came from Dr. Mesmer for a concert, and because the applause was so enormous, there were several encores. Then Baroness Waldstätten mediated some concerts for me. Everything went extremely well. In Vienna I could very quickly attract my own audience and soon would also have a nice income.

But this Archbishop (in my thoughts I call him: archrascal of an archbishop) does not permit his musicians to make a profit outside their salaries.

Then he comes up with cunning things. For example, from one moment to the next he orders a rondo for violin and orchestra. I carry out the assignment, compose, and then have to be present on the evening of the performance (it was a beautiful success, by the way) and just because of that cannot accept an invitation to an event at Countess Thun's home, where the Emperor was present. What an opportunity that would have been!

And two days ago it was suddenly – departure!

I could not do that, nor did I want to do it. I still have money to collect and for two weeks I still have concerts to perform.

So I immediately went to the Archbishop with the messenger. It was not even nine o'clock in the morning yet, but I did not let myself be stopped. I stormed into his office and asked him, still politely, for an extension of my stay in Vienna.

Things went as you can imagine, dearest Father. The Archbishop became rude. He threatened me and said that either I would travel back to Salzburg immediately, or he would deduct five hundred gilders from my pay. He called me a young rascal who does not know what privileges he enjoys at the age of twenty-five in the service of an archbishop, etc.

To that I responded to him: if Your Grace is not satisfied with me, I shall leave.

At that he flew into a total rage and screamed, "What, now the lout wants to threaten me besides?!" And he pointed me toward the door. I had already been prepared for such a reaction for a long time, and I repeated that I was terminating my service with him, and that I would bring the gilders that I had received in advance the next day.

Then the unbelievable thing happened – the secretary, Count Arco, became violent with me. He kicked me in the leg and in that manner threw me out of the Archbishop's office.

With that, my career with the Archbishop of Salzburg has come to an end once and for all.

Of course, there is also an epilogue to that violent discourse. For yesterday Count Arco came to talk with me. He said that I should reconsider the matter and come back to Salzburg after all. He, too, has often had to take acts of boorishness from the Archbishop. I said to him frankly and openly: "My dear Count Arco, you will have your reasons for swallowing acts of boorishness, and I have reasons for not swallowing them under any circumstances. For one can be a count as much as he wants to, but if he has no honor in him, he is and remains a servant."

Obviously I immediately vacated the room, and since yesterday I have been lodging with the kind Weber family. For a few weeks I shall stay with Mrs. Weber and her daughters. I also receive my food here, and she takes care of my laundry.

Dearest Father, it was necessary to report everything to you in minute detail.

With a thousand hand kisses I am

Your obedient son,
Wolfgang

From his father

Salzburg, June 10, 1781

My dear Son!

What am I supposed to say?! I am too shocked about your deed, about your decision. I expect you to correct this act of liberation, your reckless decision, and enter the service of the Archbishop again immediately.

Explain your situation to him in detailed correspondence, and he will surely grant you all artistic freedom. For my part, I shall write a letter to him and speak for you and your thirst for freedom.

I cannot say anything further about you thoughtlessness. And find your own apartment immediately. The Weber woman is a matchmaker. She wants to ensnare you with mending and egg dumplings because she still has three daughters to marry off, and they are all like that coquette Aloisia.

Unfortunately, I must say that with your temperament, which vacillates back and forth between intractability and good-heartedness, you do not spare me any worry.

Accept my fatherly embraces.

Leopold Mozart

To his father

Vienna, August 28, 1781

Dearest Father!

I can turn and twist your last letter however I want to, but I cannot recognize my father in a single line!

What sort of a father image did I have, that I assumed you would sympathize with me full of love and not only approve but also endorse my attitude toward the Archbishop?

Now I have awakened; I have a different father from the one whom I apparently dreamed up for myself.

You can be certain that I will not deviate a millimeter from my decision. On the contrary! If I happen to meet Count Arco by chance anywhere, even if it is in a concert, I shall give him back a kick in the a.... And all of the judges in this world can then indict me for that.

With regard to a new address I cannot write anything, because I still do not have my own apartment. I already had one, almost – but what a place! The stairwell was dark, even during the middle of the day; the room could be called a cubbyhole at most. In the kitchen there was a tiny window, and that window alone provided the light for three rooms. For the sake of good manners the landlady gave me orders to close the shutters if I were to change my clothes and therefore stand naked in the kitchen. Even the landlady called that apartment a rat's nest, but in spite of that she wanted her good money for it.

I fled and will find something else for myself.

I kiss your hands and am

Your obedient son,
Wolfgang Amadeus Mozart

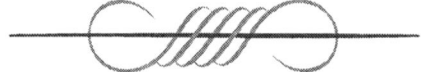

To his father

Vienna, December 16, 1781

Mon très cher Père! [My very dear Father!]

You will receive the six sonatas that were ordered in the same mail.

But now to the most important thing: I want to marry. Do not be startled at this idea of mine. I want to explain everything to you in detail.

Nature is stirring powerfully within me, but I do not want to live the way that most young men do. On the one hand I am too religious, and then I am too honest to seduce a decent girl, and I am also afraid of the diseases that attack a person who consorts with whores – I have never had anything to do with a woman of that sort. All in all I know that my temperament tends more toward the quiet and the domestic sphere. From my youth on I have simply not been accustomed to keeping my things, my underwear, my clothing, and all of the everyday affairs in order myself. It is for that reason that I am so urgently in need of a wife. Be assured, dear Father, that with a wife I will not need more money than I do in my solo life, on the contrary. I would finally like to lead an orderly life. In my eyes, a single person has only half a life – that is how I see the matter, and I have thought it out carefully.

But now, who is the object of my love? Again, do not be startled; it is a Weber girl! It is the middle one, Constanze.

Although she is the sister of Aloisia, my Constanze is simply good and sweet. I could write entire pages, but I simply want to describe her briefly. She is not ugly, but also not exactly beautiful. Her beauty consists of two small dark eyes and a beautiful figure. She has a healthy intellect and is frugal. Father, what people say is not true; she is not inclined to spend money or to extravagance. She is cleanly and makes most of the things that a woman needs for herself; she even does her own hair every day. She understands home economics and she loves me with all her heart. Could I wish for a better wife for myself?

Give me, give us your blessing.

I kiss your hands a thousand times and am

Your obedient son,
Wolf Amadé Mozart

To Constanze Weber

Vienna, April 19, 1782

Dearest, best Lady Friend!

Now consider for a moment what you have done to me! In all joviality you told me that you had a tailor measure your calves. No girl who is concerned about honor does that!

We intend to marry, after all!

Promise me once and for all that you will never again let a strange man measure your calves, and then I will no longer let my temper flare up. By the way, why are you actually so quick-tempered, for example, the day before yesterday, when I picked you up for our walk, late by half an hour after the appointed time? You know, of course, that it was because of the interview with Baroness Waldstätten, so because of my work. How angrily you reacted; you always act so gentle.

But fine, I want to forgive my Constanze and am and remain

Well-meaning and lovingly yours
Mozart

To his sister

Vienna, May 11, 1782

Dear Nannerl!

Just imagine! My Constanze's guardian came and demanded from me a written marital declaration – or I would have to give up the girl! What else could I do? I thought everything out carefully, and at the age of 26 I am not so stupid that I will simply marry on the spur of the moment. Constanze is a girl who lacks nothing but money.

In any case, I gave it to the guardian in writing that I obligate myself to marry Constanze Weber within three years, or, if I should change my mind, pay her three hundred gilders a year.

I immediately signed that document, for I know that I will never have to pay the three hundred gilders, because I shall marry my little Constanze.

Be firmly pinched and embraced by

Your brother,
Wolfgang

To his father
Vienna, June 20, 1782

Dearest Father!

I have not yet made many useful acquaintances. I am busy giving piano lessons, and that is quite a thing: the daughters endeavor to attain the correct notes and placement of their fingers and that is already punishment enough. But then I have to deal with their mothers! I am saddled with one like that now! She wants me, of all people, to perfect her piano playing. But playing the piano is only a pretext for this mother, for she wants me to sit at her side for two hours, and then she acts like she is in love! At first I thought it was a joke and did not say anything about it. But soon she took more and more liberties, and I politely told her the truth – namely that she could not continue to steal my time. The old woman was not insulted at all by that; she said, "Oh, my dear Mozart, I like you so much!"

And now she is saying everywhere that I am going away with her, and that, dear Father, I wish to set straight with this letter. I am not going away with that person, and I shall break off contact with that family immediately and avoid that foolish, infatuated woman.

And, dearest Father, whatever else is being reported to you, do not believe it. If I were to marry all of the women with whom I have laughed and whose backsides I have pinched in fun, I would probably already have two hundred wives.

As you know, my mind is inclined toward marriage – and specifically to Constanze.

With heartfelt hand kisses I am

Your obedient son,
Wolfgang

To his cousin Maria Anna Thekla Mozart

Vienna, July 3, 1782

Ma très chère Cousine! [My very dear Cousin!]

Now I can write a juicy letter to you again, and I am looking forward to that. But before I write to you I have to go to the toilet...now that is over and I feel better.

You wrote that you had headaches, a sore throat, and pain in your arm. I hope that those ailments are gone now, especially at the moment when you read my letter.

You are amazed at my bad handwriting? I want to explain it to you: When I am in a bad mood, then I write beautifully, straight, and seriously. If I am in a good mood, as I am today, then I write wildly, crooked, and funny.

Then, of course, you have more difficulty reading it, but what do you prefer? But now I ask you seriously how you are doing. Can you still like me, or are you angry with me, and I do not even know the reason? I do not want to prattle any longer, let's make peace, and in honor of it, let's let out a good fart; that will be the symbol of our peace.

You know that I shall marry in the near future; I am very happy about that and could also use a few good wishes from you. What is happening with your marriage prospect with Rudolf? Are you still putting him off? The poor man! You have mastered perfectly the virtue of delaying resistance – and I know that at your side he will do well.

Adieu ma chère Cousine [Farewell, my dear Cousin], I remain

Your faithful cousin,
Wolfgang Amadeus

To his sister Nannerl

Vienna, August 3, 1782

Dearest Sister!

The things that a person encounters. Old Mrs. Weber, my Constanze's mother, actually sent her maid to my house with the order – Constanze has to come home immediately, or her mother will have my Stanzerl picked up by the police! Are the police permitted to enter every house here in Vienna, just like that?!

You can see, dear Sister, there is only *one* means – tomorrow morning I shall marry Constanze.

I embrace you – as often as I have already taken tobacco today!

Your brother,
Wolfgang Amadé

To his father

Vienna, August 4, 1782

Mon très cher Père! [My very dear Father!]

Now it is behind us: Constanze Weber and the orchestra conductor Wolfgang Amadeus Mozart were joined in marriage, and with that my dear Constanze is now really my wife.

I thank you for your paternal blessing.

The church ceremony was so beautiful and also so modest that everyone wept, even the priest – yes, we were all very moved.

After the wedding there was a dinner in *Die Goldene Kugel* on the *Michaelerplatz*. Kind Baroness Waldstätten invited us all to it.

I am progressing steadily with my work; I am not behind with any order, and I am sending you a short march. You can give it away to somebody.

My wife and I kiss your hands many thousand times.

Your obedient son,
Wolfgang

Postscript: On our wedding day we had ideal weather — it was hot, everything was flooded with sunlight, and in the evening it rained. That is important, of course. Rain brings the blessing of children.

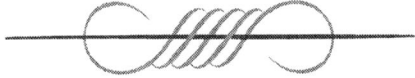

To his father

Vienna, January 6, 1783

Dearest Father!

It is miserably cold, and no matter how much we heat there is only smoke and soot, since our factotum Josef brought us damp wood. He is really a good soul, our houseman and all-purpose servant, but if a woodcutter tells him a sob story about a sick mother, he buys a handcart full of wet wood from him. And we have the smoke and the pests that are hidden in the moldering wood.

Now I do not want to tell you anything more about mundane problems, but rather I want to tell you something important, something basic: There is no future for me in Vienna of the kind that you would wish.

For no steady position in the court is in sight at all.

I must say that very clearly to you, because I read between the lines in your letters that you believe that I do not make enough effort to obtain a permanent position as the orchestra director or concert master for the good Emperor Josef II. I can twist and turn it however I want. The honorable Master Christoph Willibald Gluck and Antonio Salieri have established themselves so well at court, with all of the firm contracts, that one of them would have to die for me to have a chance.

Do not be horrified by my openness, but I can no longer hold back my resentment.

In Vienna everything proceeds by way of fraternizations and intrigues. Now a fraud has even been revealed. A few years ago, Antonio Salieri wrote an opera, *Les Danides*, for Master Gluck. And that opera was even performed in Versailles with the very greatest success, under the name of Ch. W. Gluck. Salieri directed it personally. The people were amazed – what a change in the strict style of Master Gluck, with the harmony completely in the manner of the Italian Salieri school.

In any case, the two scoundrels – or should I call them deceivers – confessed everything after the thirteenth performance. And what then occurred is unbelievable: Salieri was celebrated as if a star had fallen from the sky. Nobody at all was interested in the fact that the people had been led around by the nose for twelve performances – so enchanting was the music, supposedly. And in that way, as cunning as he is, Salieri attained everything. He has now made the good Master Gluck his accomplice, his brother. Gluck was moved, of course, by the fact that a genius like Salieri wrote an opera for him, and without any vanity at all wrote the name "Gluck" under the composition. And finally Salieri even stepped courageously and modestly – we know that charming Italian, of course – before the public and confessed his authorship. What a magnanimous deed!

And that is the way a career is made here in Vienna.

Gluck is the imperial orchestra director and Salieri is his right-hand man. They walk through the city like father and son. And if Gluck should die, Salieri already had his hand on the doorknob of the imperial court.

Dearest Father, I had to explain that to you in detail, so that you know that your remonstrations do reach me here, but that I can do nothing. The situation is as it is.

I continue to compose pieces by assignment. Countess Thun ordered a half dozen minuets for the May parade in the

Prater, and she paid in advance. So things are progressing steadily.

I kiss your hands a thousand times and beg you to take care of your health.

Your obedient son,
Wolfgang Amadeus

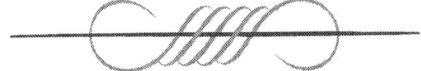

To his father

Vienna, June 17, 1783

You are a grandfather! The pains began last night at around two o'clock, and at around seven o'clock in the morning everything was over, and we have a big, strong, roly-poly boy. We want to name him Raimund Leopold, assuming that you agree, of course.

And with that I kiss your hands a thousand times and remain

Your obedient son,
Wolf Amadi

To his wife Constanze

Linz, October 30, 1783

My dearest Wife!

Just imagine, on the 4th of November I am supposed to give a concert here. They all expect something new from me, and I do not have a single symphony with me, so I am writing furiously on a new one – I am doing very well with it.

In general things are going well for me in the home of Count Anton Thun. Only you are missing. Otherwise I could work even better because I could talk with you now and then.

It is comfortably warm for me in my room; for a nightcap the maid brings me warm eggnog, and in the morning the valet rings a little silver bell. "Master Mozart, a new day has dawned again. It is five-thirty," he whispers.

He has probably already watched me and observed that in the mornings I press a few kisses onto your picture and while doing so say: "Good morning, dear little Wife! I hope that you slept well, that hopefully nothing disturbed you, that you will not hop out of bed too quickly, that you will not catch cold and will not have to be irritated with the servants. I send you many kisses! Do you feel it? Here comes another one. Did you catch it?"

Yes, my dearest Constanze, I miss you very much.

And now I shall continue to work on the new symphony.

Always yours, with love,
Wolfgang

To his sister

Vienna, May 14, 1784

My dearest Sister Heart!

We are living in terrible confusion these days, since we just moved again. Constanze wanted to move further into the inner city, and I could never deny a wish to her. You know, of course, that we are expecting our second child in October.

So I am sitting surrounded by heaps of laundry, two baskets of potatoes, and stacks of sheets of music, and I can actually find no peace at all to work. Therefore I am writing a letter to you now, because you should be informed about some things anyway. And later I shall continue to work on the two sonatas that were ordered.

Nannerl, nothing is going according to my plan in Vienna.

I must pour out my heart to you. A permanent position at court is unattainable for me as long as Antonio Salieri goes in and out there. He simply has the more favorable way of presenting himself; he also has more time for salon life than I do. With his annual salary he does not have to depend on assignment work. My household fund is constantly empty, although I earn well. But the household expenses for a family are quite high. Our dear Papa would say that we should economize more – well, just where, just how? The three servants come punctually every four weeks with their little pay books, and now and then I need a new shirt and new pants, and my piano must often be repaired because it is damaged almost every time it is transported. My dear Constanze needs the least amount. She mends her stockings; she turns her dresses and with a few galloons she conjures new ones from them.

Now I have a request for you: could you encourage our dear father to visit us sometime in Vienna. If he sees how well Constanze and I live with each other, if he sees how modest my Constanze is, then he will change his opinion about her.

For, the fact that Papa rejects my Constanze so stubbornly – that hurts me.

So, dear Sister, help ease this sore spot for me.

By the way, I have almost exclusively noble ladies as students, Countess Rumbeck, Countess Palffy, Lady von Trattner. And a month ago Princess Elisabeth von Württemberg wrote to me that she wanted to become my student. She would have paid an enormously high honorarium; but Salieri was faster than I was. He sent her a perfumed note as a welcoming greeting, and now she is his student. He is more adroit in everything.

Now I shall close this letter and sprinkle a few drops of lavender water on it, all for you, dear little Sister.

I send you heartfelt greetings and embraces.

Your brother,
Wolferl

A postscript: Today is a midsummer's day of the kind that I especially like; it is so comfortably warm that I can work all night with the window open.

To his sister

Vienna, August 12, 1784

Ma très chère sour! [My very dear Sister!] Dear Nannerl!

Now it really is time for me to write, if I want my letter to reach you while you are still a virgin. A few days more and it will be too late.

My wife and I wish you every happiness in your change of status and heartily regret that we cannot be present at your wedding. We hope, however, to be able to embrace you and your husband, Johann von Berchthold zu Sonnenberg, in St. Gilgen next spring. We feel sorry, of course, for our dear father, who will now live all alone. Of course, you are not all too far away from him, and he can often come and visit you.

Now I send you a thousand good wishes from Vienna to Salzburg, above all that the two of you will live together as well as the two of us do.

And take from my poetic head one more little piece of advice:

In marriage you will experience much that was halfway puzzling to you. You will soon know from experience how Eve had to act so that she gave birth to a child afterward. But Sister, you will very gladly carry out those marital duties, for, believe me, they are not difficult. But everything has two sides. Marriage brings many pleasures, to be sure, but it also brings grief. Therefore, when your husband gives you a black look and is in a bad mood, just think that it is a man's whim and say to yourself: let his will be done during the day and mine at night.

Receive hearty embraces from

Your brother,
Wolf Amadi

To his wife Constanze

Prague, December 4, 1784

Dearest little Wife!

If only I had a letter from you! If I were to tell you everything that I do with your dear portrait, you would probably laugh often. For example, when I take it out of its case, I say: "Hello, Stanzerl!" And when I put it back, then I say: "Good night, little mouse, and sleep well."

So I just write stupid things to you, but they are only stupid for the world; for us, however, who love each other so deeply, it is certainly not stupid. Today is the sixth day that I have been away from you, and it seems to me as if it were already a year. You will have difficulty reading my letter because I am in a hurry and am therefore writing poorly. Farewell my love, my only woman. I kiss you millions of times and am eternally

Your loving husband,
W. A. Mozart

Father Leopold Mozart to his daughter Nannerl

Vienna, March 14, 1785

Dear Daughter!

My visit to your brother will end in a week, and I want to convey my impressions to you.

Wolfgang works like a berserker. He has the mornings reserved for students, and he has only students from noble circles, students who pay well. Then he is obligated for subscription concerts, for salon parties in the royal houses, sometimes as the director, sometimes as a soloist on the piano. During the last month, for example, he gave concerts 26 times.

For those, of course, he also has to write new things, and only the night is left to him for that, for in the afternoons he must practice, write his correspondence, and keep appointments for dinner. All in all, during the two months that I have been here, he has earned almost six hundred gilders, of which he can put a nice sum in Rothschild's bank; and if he continues to be so industrious, he will have a secure future

But – his household! Constanze does not understand much about the management of household affairs. She keeps three servants, of whom none really works; the cook loafs around and sends the valet to the restaurant for a dumpling soup instead of cooking something himself!

With all of this disorder I am amazed that Wolfgang can work at all. And with that I come to Constanze as a wife. I have been able to convince myself of this fact – Constanze is actually the wife that he needs. She is devoted, embraces him at every opportunity, dances with him, and is enthusiastic about the smallest chord that he composes. She warms his underwear; she cuts his meat for him; she brings him a new warm brick for his feet every two hours, and when he nods off over his work, then she massages his neck and back – above all she is always cheerful. She never complains, even when he often does not come home until after midnight, even when his patrons owe him money. She is really a very modest, special person, and for Wolfgang, for his work, she is a blessing.

Constanze is certainly by far the best woman from her family. For her mother, Cäcilia Weber, is a real monster who constantly asks Wolfgang for money. Sometimes for the doctor because of her varicose veins, then for a laundry tub, then for a cure in Baden, then for dancing lessons for her youngest daughter – and Wolfgang pays and gives. He does not have time at all to keep track of the money that has been begged from him.

His works will soon be extensive enough that people will no longer be able to overlook him in the encyclopedias. Even if they do write in the *Magazin für Musik*: "Mozart does have an inclination toward the brilliant and unusual, but actually his compositions have little high culture. The technical element is missing from his compositions."

In that regard it is good that Wolfgang has no time to read such things. For that would hurt him, and how could we console him?

By the way, Wolfgang and I are now members, "fellows," of the Free Mason lodge *Zur gekrönten Hoffnung* [New Crowned Hope]. The kind Count von Born opened the door to that lodge for Wolfgang, and as you know, I have always supported the efforts of the Free Masons. For, what can a reasonable person want more than fraternal equal rights, benevolent building of a better world, and the combating of superstition?

My dear Daughter, I am looking forward to our reunion, to your orderly world, to your delicious food, and naturally to your piano playing.

Receive hearty embraces from
Your father

To his wife Constanze

Berlin, February 1, 1786

My dear little Wife!

When I return, you really must look forward more to *me*, and not to the money! I am not bringing 900 thalers, but only 700; the money dwindled because I had to pay for my own food in the expensive town of Potsdam. There I also had to loan Lichnovsky a hundred thalers because he was running out of money, and you know how that is; I could scarcely deny it to him.

The musical program in Leipzig went badly, as expected, but I shall tell you about that in person.

Be satisfied with what I am bringing.

In only four days I shall be with my dearest little wife.

Yours,
Wolfgang

To his sister
Vienna, May 26, 1787

Dear Nannerl!

What you write about our dear Papa gives me cause for great concern, for I do not believe that our father is at all accustomed to accepting attacks of weakness; therefore he also does not tolerate them in other people.

Play for him as often as possible, for your piano playing has always cheered him up. You have that wonderful soft touch; Papa was especially proud of that and is undoubtedly still proud of it today.

Otherwise, I cannot do anything, for it is impossible for me to leave Vienna, for in a short time my students would find themselves another teacher, and I depend on that income.

By the way, for two weeks I had a young musician with me under contract; he came from Bonn, Ludwig van Beethoven. A very talented seventeen-year-old, but drilled too much by his musical parents. Every tone, every gesture hammered in to perfection, but there was no recognizable melody – in that respect technical matters and drill really are not the essence of music, but only the melody is the essence of music. After a week he freely improvised on the piano for the first time, and that was extremely beautiful. He, himself, was moved to tears, because in the process something opened up inside him.

I would have liked to have continued working with that student; the Elector of Bonn paid for him personally. But unfortunately Beethoven's mother became seriously ill and he had to return to Germany.

As you can read, things are going moderately well. The money comes in, the money flies out, and we never have a thing in the cash box.

But I have my work.

Be heartily embraced by

Your brother,
Wolfgang

To his sister

Vienna, June 17, 1787

Dear Nannerl!

Barely an hour ago we returned from Prague and I found your letter waiting – we no longer have a father.

I cannot say anything at all about that. Nor can I imagine our dear Papa lifeless, because I live in constant dialogue with him. And now all the distance has disappeared; that is why our dear Papa and I are now so close to each other. Now he understands everything, even those things that he did not want to accept in this life. Now only the truth counts anymore, specifically the truth of our hearts.

Children always lie to their parents in certain areas; that is the only way it can be. The parents do not want to let go of their wish image, and their children do not want to disappoint them.

And our friend, Death, puts all of that right. Now all that is left is closeness and intimacy.

Dear Nannerl, it is comforting that you write that our father passed peacefully away in his sleep.

I have wept a great deal recently; that is perhaps the case because I am so tired and the smallest event, the laughter of our little Carl or a brief improvisation on the piano immediately causes me to become intensely emotional. Only when I work, then things go well for me – and I have a lot of work to do, of course.

Accept my firm, brotherly embraces and let us comfort each other that way.

Your brother,
Wolfgang

To his friend Michael Puchberg

Vienna, July 4, 1788

My dear, best friend, Michael!

Your true friendship makes me so bold as to involve you in my private business. But you have known me since my first days in Vienna in the year 1781, when I was permitted to give a concert in your salon and in that manner was able to get out of a commitment to the Archbishop.

You are familiar with the fact that following the death of Master Gluck – whom I revered very much – in January of this year, I received the position of a royal and imperial chamber musician. How relieved I was at that appointment – a fixed annual salary at last.

However – while Master Gluck received two thousand gilders, they pay me only eight hundred. You, as a merchant, will see at a glance and say: That is not just. But in this matter I have no desire, for Gluck was a man of world renown, and in my case they say that I must still make an effort to obtain respect. What answer should I have given to the secretary in the court music office, when he said to me: "You are certainly very diligent, but the Viennese are not really very enthusiastic about your music. Give some thought to what you could do to become famous – then you will certainly receive a full salary."

In any case, it is a fact that for two years I have been living in serious financial difficulties. The rent constantly gets higher, and because we were behind in our rent payments we had to move to *Währingerstrasse*. We now live more closely confined, but I do not want to complain about that. But I still have repair expenses for the pianoforte – for that reason I summon all my courage to ask you for a loan. I think of one or two thousand gilders; then I could dispose of all of my open bills and begin with a clean slate.

To tell you the truth, I do not know what else to do, for without help I cannot put things in order, and my dear Constanze has no talent for money matters.

If you cannot help me with such a large sum, then I ask you to lend me a few hundred gilders and to identify a person for me who will give a larger amount against documents and my signature.

Now I want to stop this stammering, but without the necessary money one is a hopeless creature. I always live between hope and fear, but that is the lot of the independent artist.

Very honestly and affectionately yours,
Wolfgang Amadé

To his wife Constanze

Vienna, September 16, 1788

Dearest, best little Wife of my heart!

Now you have only been away for a few hours on your way to Baden, and I already can no longer stand it. I must talk with you.
Oh, Stanzerl, we are in such a miserable situation. The Lord God took our little Reserl to himself. When I prick up my ears, I think that I can still hear her happy laughter. And suddenly that light was extinguished. I cannot find any words for it.
Stanzerl, Fate means it so ill with us regarding our children. Of four only Carl remains to us. How can I give comfort when I find no solace myself and would almost like to be angry with Heaven? I wrote a symphony for our little girl, so that she will have a good time in heaven. I shall call this piece of music the *Jupiter Symphony*. Jupiter will surely be a benefactor to our Reserl.

My dearest little Wife, do get some rest and have a good cry. Tears are the best medicine for such a blow of Fate.

Eternally yours,
Mozart

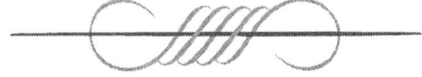

To his wife Constanze

Prague, March 1, 1789

Dearest little Wife!

I received your dear letter with pleasure. Tomorrow morning I shall depart, and soon we will embrace each other; and believe me, I am traveling only to see you again. For they will soon be performing *Figaro* here, and there are some changes that need to be made, and accordingly I am needed at the rehearsals. But I shall arrange everything with respect to time.

Now I want to speak to you honestly. You write that you are sad, and behind your words I read that you do not trust me? Because there is so much talk, of course, and especially because of Nancy Storace! You do not have any reason to worry. You have a husband who loves you, who lays everything possible at your feet.

But since I am speaking so frankly – I am pleased, of course, if you are happy in Baden, but I simply do not want you to waste your time with just anybody. A woman must always merit respect and remain reserved, otherwise she is talked about! So do not be too intimate. Be happy and cheerful, but do not torment me with your jealousy, and believe me: only the clever behavior of a woman can put chains on a man.

Farewell. Tomorrow I shall kiss you heartily.

Yours,
Wolfgang

To his friend Michael Puchberg

Vienna, September 21, 1789

My best, understanding friend! Dear Michael!

With this letter I wanted to thank you for the generous help that you accorded to me half a year ago. And now I am not only *unable* to repay you, but must submit a new request.

I beg you for some support, in whatever amount you deign to give, for I do not have a single gilder. A month ago I gave the publisher Artaria three new quartets; he paid me a ridiculously small sum for them. I cannot complain about that, for when one is in extreme need, as I am, one must take what one receives. And with the money from Artaria I was able to save our large dinner table, for I cannot take that table to a pawn shop, because I urgently need it to work on. Süssmayr (first he was my student and now he is my assistant) copies my notes and my scores on it, and I, too, need the table, since my desk is not big enough for my work; I am constantly composing several pieces simultaneously.

Visit me sometime; see for yourself how I live, that any luxury is absent here. Yesterday the large music cabinet was taken to the pawn shop. Perhaps I can buy it back.

I am filled with black thoughts; you are the only one I tell that, and I can only drive away that darkness in my soul with work. The kind Franz Demel gave me a loan of 100 gilders; his wife is my student. With that money I could travel to Berlin; perhaps there I will receive the commission for a major opera.

Accept my friendly and hearty embrace, and I implore you once more for your help.

Yours,
Wolfgang Amadé

To his friend Michael Puchberg

Vienna, May 16, 1790

My dearest friend, dear Michael!

For a few weeks I had the hope that my luck would change. For in October, as you know, the coronation of our Emperor Leopold II will take place. The most important chamber musicians will accompany him, and I admit that I firmly counted on an invitation. But for Antonio Salieri – he determines which musicians go – as the third orchestra conductor I am much too low in station.

That invitation did not come.

I am very grieved about that, for I know that it would be very important to be in Frankfurt. I would surely receive commissions and also be able to give concerts.

This constant paying off of debts in installments burdens my soul. They recently raised the rent, and I do not have to write to you about the price of wood; following the last severe winter they have been charging for pieces of wood as if they were gold bars. Sometimes I fear that I will become ill, for my weariness and my headaches do not diminish. But I shall not permit illness, never!

I must push aside my worries with even more discipline, and when I work all night for a few nights, then I am exhausted, to be sure, but I feel better.

With all affection and gratitude I am

Your devoted friend,
Wolfgang Amadeus

To his wife Constanze

Frankfurt, October 3, 1790

My very dearest little Wife, Constanzerl!

The trip was short, but my behind is sore anyway. And now I am sitting in a hole of a room, the cheapest one that I could obtain. I have already received commissions to conduct and to play solos. I want to inform you of that quickly. I intend only to work and to work, and soon things will go better for us.

I send you a thousand kisses, always with love

Yours,
Wolfgang

To his wife Constanze

Frankfurt, October 17, 1790

Dearest little wife, my dearest Constanzerl!

    This trip was not the right thing after all, for ostentation is the only dominant thing here. People make promises to me from all sides, say to me that I am a famous man – but the money does not come, and even if I am paid for a concert, then very meagerly.

    In the next few days I shall flee from here by the cheapest coach. Look, now a tear has fallen on the paper. We will not despair, my dear.

    So many dear words and caresses are flying around – now I have caught hold of an embrace from you, and another one! Yes, I feel you quite tangibly.

    With many thousands of kisses I am

Yours,
Wolfgang

To his friend Michael Puchberg

Vienna, May 20, 1791

My dear friend Michael!

    Today I am not asking you for money again but for patience. I still cannot repay anything, because I immediately had to give the honorarium that I received for my last two sonatas to the landlord – the rent!

At this time I am busy working on a major opera. Emmanuel Schikaneder, a theater man whom I know from Salzburg, gave me an opera libretto. It is a fairy tale opera in which a magic flute plays the central role. It is a work that I am really enjoying, and although we did not agree to any deadline at all, I am composing almost day and night.

Usually I work in Schikaneder's summerhouse. There it is more comfortable for me, for my Constanzerl is in Baden with our little Carl. Süssmayr and Josef do keep the house clean, but the food is usually cold when they bring it from the restaurant; often the water jugs are empty and they are unwilling to heat the place because they to not want to accept the fact that I am freezing although it is already May. By contrast, at Schikaneder's things are comfortable for me; he brings the pot of hot soup to my desk, and in the afternoon I even receive black coffee.

My dearest, brotherly friend, I ask you for your patience. As soon as I can I shall begin repaying my debts to you.

With sincere and heart affection I am

Yours,
Wolfgang Amadé

To his wife Constanze

Vienna, June 2, 1791

My dearest little Wife!

I have just this minute received your letter, and I already long for the next one in order to learn how much good the

water cure is doing you. I also regret that I was not present at your beautiful music performance yesterday, but not because of the music, rather because I would then have been so happy to be with you. Do not forget my warning about the morning and evening air, and also about bathing too long. I send you a thousand kisses and am
Eternally yours,
Wolfgang

P.S.: *Perhaps it would be good to give our little Carl a bit more fruit. And get a proper amount of sleep, Stanzerl! You must remain healthy, otherwise I worry.*

How is our next baby doing? If he kicks hard, good for him, or her.

Again a thousand kisses,

Yours,
Wolferl

To his wife Constanze

Vienna, September 10, 1791

Dearest, best little Wife!

With the greatest joy I found your letter when I returned from the opera!

I just ate a nice piece of rabbit; perhaps I will have some more brought, for today I have quite an appetite. It occurs to me that it is probably the case because I forgot to eat anything yesterday. I composed until two in the morning, then I straightened up my desk, and then it was already time for my morning coffee.

Then I immediately went to the opera house and played Papageno's chimes for them myself – and that was a good thing, because suddenly they understood everything. After that I was at Schikaneder's again; he offered me wine, but I did not want anything to eat. Yes, and that is how the hours pass.

Look, now I have interrupted the letter for two days. I have not slept well. In general, my best little Wife, it is the case that I have somehow lost track of time – when it is day and when it is night. I am simply always sitting at the table writing and composing. There is confusion inside me and I can hardly put it on paper. I want to write everything down simultaneously and in the process my hours pass, and then the day slides into the night, and I hardly look up again and it is another day already. Since a stack of sheets covered with writing lies in front of me, however, I probably did not sleep. That is how it goes, Stanzerl, when you are not here. So come soon, and hopefully well.

By the way, I have been looking for my yellow winter pants for days now. Did you send them to the laundry? Josef cannot find them either.

Farewell, I am so tired.

Eternally yours,
Wolferl

P.S.: Xaver Süssmayr is an important support to me; I should pay him for his copy work and for his assistance with all the writing tasks. But when, and how much?

To his wife Constanze

Vienna, September 20, 1791

My dearest little Wife!

    You do not like it at all when I talk about dying, because you have such a fear of death. I confess that I cannot understand that at all, for I have no fear of cousin Death. I am often so tired that I would like to stagger toward him. There he stands, at the gate to the other, to the better world, and beyond it is only happiness. He has already been my best friend for many years. His image has nothing terrifying for me, only a calming and comforting influence. I think that to entrust oneself to him and to walk hand in hand with him through the gate is the actual purpose of our lives. But until then we still have so much to do, and it must all be done, and it is not for us to ask – why and how it is so.
    Accept a million kisses,

Eternally yours,
Wolfgang Amadé Mozart

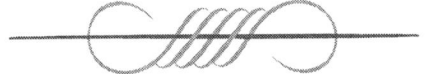

To his friend Michael Puchberg

Vienna, October 7, 1791

Dearest brotherly friend Puchberg!

I would gladly follow your advice and recuperate or at least work less hours. How am I supposed to do that? Rest wearies and exhausts me much more than composing; my mind is then quite confused from resting. No, for me it is better to compose. I have nothing more to tremble about and for that reason I am also no longer sad; although I often weep, but that is more because my eyes are tired. Life really has been beautiful, and my career began in such a promising manner. But a person cannot alter his destiny.

Of course I understand your rebuke, that I have been too careless and not ambitious enough about presenting my name properly on the theater program and putting it in the right light. You say that would reduce the importance of my name, of my work. Perhaps.

For me the period of work on this opera was a good period; I did not perceive anything around me but only lived for that opera. And as weary as I am, to put it honestly, it is immaterial to me that on the theater program it says: *"The Magic Flute"* (*Die Zauberflöte*), a grand opera by Emmanuel Schikaneder." It is also written there, even though it is in small print: "The music is by Mr. Wolfgang Amadeus Mozart."

If it really should be as you fear, that I wind up in conflict with Schikaneder because of the gilders, then I trust that you will take on this matter. I have no strength for a legal battle over money.

Supposedly the opera will be performed another dozen times. Perhaps money will actually come in! You will please be of help to my Constanze in managing the money. Do not be startled at such thoughts from me, but I feel plainly that I will soon have written my last music. I am always cold, while we are really having a beautiful, warm autumn.

Dearest friend, accept my deepest and my honest thanks.

Yours,
Wolfgang Amadé

To his wife Constanze

Vienna, October 31, 1791

My dearest little Wife!

There was a man here yesterday who gave me an urgent assignment. He was a remarkable figure, not at all talkative, but he placed a full leather bag on the table. I immediately asked what he would like – dance music, perhaps something for a wedding dinner, or a lively march, perhaps a sonata or a heart-stirring minuet?

But he, this visitor, this customer, shook his head at everything and said only, "A requiem." And I was hardly able to ask for whom it was to be, and whether it should be with or without a chorus. Then he said only, "Quickly, Mozart, there is not much time left. I shall have the score picked up during the first days of December," and then he was gone.

You will not believe it, Stanzerl, but now I do not even know the name of that customer. But he was quite obviously serious, for he did leave me the leather bag full of money.

Oh, well, so I shall simply write a requiem and while doing so imagine that I am writing it for a person of very high station. For he must be a member of the nobility, the way he talked with me like somebody from another world. This man is certainly not from Vienna; I know all of the nobility there.

That was a peculiar visit. Somehow he was not at all a stranger to me. Do I know him from somewhere? Stanzerl, come home. I am so tired; I am now seeing strange things everywhere.

Eternally and lovingly your Wolferl,
Wolfgang Amadeus Mozart

Five weeks later, on the 5th of December 1791, Wolfgang Amadeus Mozart died of rheumatic fever, he was about thirty-six.
The requiem was unfinished.
The customer for the requiem was Count Walsegg-Stuppach of Lower Austria.

THE MOZART FAMILY

Father: Leopold Mozart

Born on November 14, 1719 in Augsburg, Germany, had three brothers and one sister; his father was a book binder; his mother was a housewife.

Leopold Mozart was educated in a Jesuit school, studied philosophy in Salzburg, began to compose at an early age, had a perfect command of the violin, and became a violinist in the court orchestra of the Archbishop at the age of 24. He wrote books of music and music textbooks, e.g. *Die gründliche Violinschule* (The Basic Violin Method).

Married Anna Maria Pertl on November 21, 1747.

He died on May 28, 1787 in Salzburg.

Mother: Anna Maria Mozart, née Pertl

Born on December 25, 1719 in St. Gilgen, Austria, no siblings; her father was a lawyer; her mother was a housewife.

When Anna Maria was four years old, her father died and her mother experienced financial difficulties. A petition for aid from the Archbishop's court ministry made it possible for Anna Maria to be educated in the lyceum.

Married Leopold Mozart on November 21, 1747.

She died on July 3, 1778, in Paris.

Children of Leopold and Anna Maria Mozart

August 1748	Johann Joachim, died in infancy.
June 1749	Maria Anna Cordula, died in infancy.
May 1750	Maria Anna Walburga, died in infancy.
July 31, 1751	Maria Anna Ignatia, "Nannerl," died October 29, 1829 at the age of 78 years.
November 1752	Johann Karl, died in infancy.
January 27, 1756	*Johannes Chrysostomus Wolfgangus Theophilus, called Wolfgang Amadeus,* died December 5, 1791 in Vienna at the age of 36 years.

Sister: "Nannerl", Maria Anna Ignatia Mozart

Born on July 31, 1751 in Salzburg; married Johann Baptist von Berchthold zu Sonnenberg on August 1784.

Children:	1785	Leopold
	1789	Johanna
	1790	Marie Babette (died in infancy)

Nannerl gave piano lessons. In the year 1820 she became blind. Died on October 29, 1829 in Salzburg.

Wife: Constanze Mozart, née Weber

Born on January 5, 1762 in Zell, Black Forest, Germany. Her father, Franz Fridolin Weber, was a town clerk and music copyist; her mother was a housewife.

Constanze's sisters: Aloisia, singer,
                       Josepha, singer,
                       Sophie, housewife

After the death of Wolfgang Amadeus Mozart, Constanze's second marriage – in the year 1809 to Georg Nikolaus von Nissen, a Danish government official and Mozart's first biographer; in 1826 Constanze became a widow for the second time; she died March 6, 1842 in Salzburg.

Little cousin: Maria Anna Thekla Mozart

Born on September 25, 1758 in Augsburg; remained unmarried; had a daughter out of wedlock (born 1784); died in 1841 in Bayreuth, Germany.

Chronology of Mozart's Private Life

January 27, 1756	Johannes Chrysostomus Wolfgangus Theophilus Mozart is born in Salzburg.
July 3, 1778	Mozart's mother, Anna Maria Mozart, née Pertl, dies in Paris at the age of 58 years.
August 4, 1782	Marriage to Constanze Weber.
June 17, 1783	Birth of his son, Raimund Leopold, who dies September 18, 1783.
September 21, 1784	Birth of his son, Carl Thomas, who dies in 1858 at the age of 74 years.
October 18, 1786	Birth of his son, Johann Thomas Leopold, who dies in November 1786.
December 27, 1787	Birth of his daughter, Theresia Constantia Adelheid (Reserl), who dies in June 1788.
November 16, 1789	Birth of his daughter, Anna Maria, who dies immediately after birth.

July 26, 1791   Birth of his son, Franz Xaver Wolfgang, who dies in 1844 at the age of 53 years.

December 5, 1791   Wolfgang Amadeus Mozart dies in Vienna of rheumatic fever and is buried in an unmarked grave in the St. Marx Cemetery in Vienna.

GLOSSARY

Members of royalty whom Mozart knew personally

    Maria Theresia, Empress of Austria
    Josef II, Emperor of Austria
    Marie Antoinette, Queen of France

    Pope Clemens XIV

Friends of Mozart

    Johann Becke, flutist
    Baroness Elisabeth Waldstätten
    Franz Xaver Süssmayr, student and music copyist
    Michael Puchberg, merchant

Composers

    Christoph Willibald Gluck (1714-1787)
    Antonio Salieri (1750-1825)
    Niccolo Piccini (1728-1800)

Additional Individuals

>Jeanne Antoinette Poisson de Pompadour, mistress of Louis XV
>
>Marie Jeanne Dubarry, a favorite of Louis XV
>
>Melchior Grimm, secretary of the Duke of Orleans and a friend of Wolfgang's father Leopold Mozart
>
>Thresel, cook and housemaid
>
>Rosl, laundress
>
>Ignaz, house servant
>
>Emanuel Schikaneder, theater director and librettist
>
>Ludwig van Beethoven (1770-1827)